Frank Muir
on Children

By the Same Author
The Frank Muir Book

Frank Muir
on Children

Frank Muir and Simon Brett

Research by Virginia Bell

Illustrated by
Joseph Wright

Heinemann : London

William Heinemann Ltd
10 Upper Grosvenor Street, London W1X 9PA
LONDON MELBOURNE TORONTO
JOHANNESBURG AUCKLAND

First published 1980
© Text: Frank Muir, Simon Brett and Virginia Bell 1980
© Illustrations: Joseph Wright 1980
434 48151 3

Frank Muir on Children is inspired
by the Yorkshire Television series
of the same name.

Phototypeset in V.I.P. Palatino by
Western Printing Services Ltd, Bristol
Printed in Great Britain
at The Pitman Press, Bath

contents

1

little devils

Children have always aroused strong emotional reactions. And one has to face the fact that a lot of people just DO NOT LIKE THEM. Here are a few opinions from the anti-child faction. First, one quoted by Dr Johnson:

> One cannot love lumps of flesh, and little infants are nothing more.

Fran Lebowitz:

> Even when freshly washed and relieved of all obvious confections, children tend to be sticky.

W. C. Fields:

> Anybody who hates children and dogs can't be all bad.

And it was Fields who always produced the same reply to the reporter's question, How do you like children?

FRIED.

But why do children provoke such violent distaste? A cynic would say you have only to try and live with one for any length of time to answer that question. But the reaction has been rationalized in many ways. In a primitive sense, the presence of a younger generation is a potential threat to the existing order. In their children tribal leaders see their eventual usurpers. But there are other reasons to distrust them. If you believe in Original Sin, as the Puritans of the Reformation did, children are living embodiments of evil. This is what

2

Calvin wrote on the subject in 1535:

> Yea, and very infants themselves bring their
> own damnation with them from their
> mother's womb. Who, although they have not
> yet brought forth the fruits of their iniquity,
> yet have the seed thereof inclosed within
> them. Yea, their whole nature is a certain seed
> of Sin, therefore it cannot but be hateful and
> abominable to God.

But even without the justifications of religion, it is easy to find arguments against children. Particularly babies. Babies mean a lot to their parents, but to the objective outsider, they do present certain inconveniences. Here are a couple of definitions, the first by Ambrose Bierce:

> BABE or BABY, n. A misshapen creature of
> no particular age, sex or condition, chiefly
> remarkable for the violence of the sympathies
> and antipathies it excites in others, itself
> without sentiment or emotion.

And a terser one from Father Ronald Knox:

> BABY – A loud noise at one end and no sense
> of responsibility at the other.

Benjamin Haydon, in a letter of 1825, brought a proper note of apology to the subject:

3

You have such a horror, a Malthusian horror,
of the increase of population, that I dread to
write we have been guilty here of that
abominable crime – of bringing another little
snoozling rogue into being. They both are
well, and I hope will continue so. I think
myself lucky she had not twins, for I dreaded
it most abominably.

Jane Austen, writing to her sister Cassandra in 1801,
demonstrated her customary perspicacity:

The house seemed to have all the comforts of
little children, dirt and litter.

But then that's all outsiders see. To the new mother
and father, Dickens's words remain true:

4

Every baby born into the world is a finer one than the last.

Finer, maybe, but not necessarily more beautiful. In 'Sonny Boy', a short story by P. G. Wodehouse, Bingo Little faces parenthood:

When, in the second year of his marriage to Rosie M. Banks, the eminent female novelist, his union was blessed and this bouncing boy appeared on the London scene, Bingo's reactions were, I gather, very much the same as yours. Introduced to the child in the nursing home, he recoiled with a startled 'Oi!' and, as the days went by, the feeling that he had run up against something red-hot in no way diminished.

The only thing that prevented a father's love from faltering was the fact that there was in his possession a photograph of himself at

the same early age, in which he, too, looked like a homicidal fried egg. This proof that it was possible for a child, in spite of a rocky start, to turn eventually into a suave and polished boulevardier with finely chiselled features heartened him a good deal, causing him to hope for the best.

A father's reaction to his offspring is traditionally less besotted than that of a mother. But all mothers aren't besotted to the same degree. Here's the opinion of Queen Augusta, George II's wife, of her son Frederick:

> My dear first-born is the greatest ass, and the greatest liar, and the greatest *canaille*, and the greatest beast in the whole world, and I most heartily wish he was out of it.

No, you don't always find love of children where perhaps you should expect it. Many of those who write for children are notoriously unenthusiastic about their public. Here's part of a letter by Charles Dodgson (or Lewis Carroll):

> I sent 'Sylvie and Bruno' to an Oxford friend, and, in writing his thanks, he added, 'I think I must bring my little boy to see you.' So I wrote to say *don't*.

And how about lovable old Edward Lear? Here's an extract from one of his letters:

> I was much distressed by next door people
> who had twin babies and played the violin:
> But one of the twins died, and the other has
> eaten the fiddle – so all is peace.

Some people would like to have nothing to do with children at all until they're mature. Here's the opinion of one Fergusson, quoted by James Boswell in the late eighteenth century:

> Till a child is four years old it is no better than
> a cabbage.

But a fairly noisy cabbage. Children are not very good at being unobtrusive, and their parents are always aware of their presence – particularly during school holidays. Here are two extracts from the diary of the Rev. W. J. Temple. First, the entry for 23 June, 1796:

> Laura returned in the evening from Falmouth. Rude and disagreeable ... Octavius' propensity to perverseness must be checked. Children when young are always bickering. To be a parent without an assistant is a hard task. Always doing something to discompose and interrupt tranquillity.

Three weeks later, 13 July, 1796:

> Am discomposed with Octavius, who grows very rude and troublesome. Holidays too long.

Evelyn Waugh's diary also revealed himself to have strong views on the subject of children. Here is the entry for 31 August, 1945:

> The boy Auberon stayed a week at Ickleford and won golden opinions on all sides, even mine, so that I was encouraged to have him for a few days in London and show him some sights.
> On the day we returned, Wednesday, I took him to the Zoo, which was crowded with the

lower classes and practically devoid of animals except rabbits and guinea pigs. On Friday I devoted the day to him, hiring a car to fetch him from Highgate and to return him there. I wore myself out for his amusement, taking him up the dome of St. Paul's, buying him three-cornered postage stamps and austerity toys, showing him London from the top of the hotel, taking him to tea with Mamie, who gave him a sovereign and a box of variegated matches. Finally, when I took him back to Highgate, my mother said, 'Have you had a lovely day?'

'A bit dull.'

So I felt absolved from paying further attention to him.

In literature the distaste of natural parents for their offspring is nothing to that of step-parents. In Charles Dickens's *David Copperfield*, David has the grim Mr Murdstone in this rôle, and his prospects deteriorate further with the arrival of his stepfather's sister:

It was Miss Murdstone who was arrived, and a gloomy-looking lady she was; dark, like her brother, whom she greatly resembled in face and voice, and with very heavy eyebrows, nearly meeting over her large nose, as if, being disabled by the wrongs of her sex from wearing whiskers, she had carried them to that account. She brought with her two uncompromising hard black boxes, with her initials on the lids in hard brass nails. When she paid the coachman she took her money out of a hard steel purse, and she kept the purse in a very jail of a bag which hung upon her arm by a heavy chain, and shut up like a bite. I had never, at that time, seen such a metallic lady altogether as Miss Murdstone was.

She was brought into the parlour with many tokens of welcome, and there formally recognized my mother as a new and near relation. Then she looked at me, and said:

'Is that your boy, sister-in-law?'

My mother acknowledged me.

'Generally speaking,' said Miss Murdstone, 'I don't like boys. How d'ye do, boy?'

Under these encouraging circumstances, I replied that I was very well, and that I hoped she was the same; with such indifferent grace, that Miss Murdstone disposed of me in two words:

'Wants manner!'

Miss Murdstone was not alone in her dislike of boys. Over the years a good few rude things have been said about them. This is Leslie Stephen's view from 1879:

The genus boy seems to me one of nature's mistakes. Girls improve as they grow up; but the boy generally deteriorates.

The Rev. Sydney Smith:

> I am glad it is a girl: all little boys ought to be
> shot.

Charles Lamb:

> Boys are capital fellows in their own way,
> among their mates; but they are unwholesome
> companions for grown people.

Ambrose Bierce:

> The fact that boys are allowed to exist at all is evidence of a remarkable Christian forbearance among men.

Girls haven't fared a lot better. Here's an English proverb:

> Daughters and dead fish are no keeping wares.

A thought from Christopher Morley:

> Few girls are as well shaped as a good horse.

Here's Lord Byron's view of adolescent girls, from his poem 'Beppo', published in 1818:

> 'Tis true, your budding Miss is very charming,
>   But shy and awkward at first coming out,
> So much alarmed, that she is quite alarming,
>   All Giggle, Blush; half Pertness, and half
>   Pout;
> And glancing at Mamma, for fear there's harm
>   in
>   What you, she, it, or they, may be about,
> The nursery still lisps in all they utter –
> Besides, they always smell of bread and
>   butter.

An accusation that is levelled at children of both sexes

12

is that they are awful and impossible to live with. In O. Henry's short story 'The Ransom of Red Chief', two kidnappers snatch a truly awful child and demand fifteen hundred dollars from the boy's father, and this is the reply they receive:

> Gentlemen: I received your letter today by post, in regard to the ransom you ask for the return of my son. I think you are a little high in your demands, and I hereby make you a counter-proposition, which I am inclined to believe you will accept. You bring Johnny home and pay me two hundred and fifty dollars in cash, and I agree to take him off your hands. You had better come at night, for the neighbours believe he is lost, and I couldn't be responsible for what they would do to anybody they saw bringing him back.
> Very respectfully, Ebenezer Dorset.

Here's another appalling child from a Ruthless Rhyme by Harry Graham, entitled 'Quiet Fun':

> My son Augustus, in the street one day,
>   Was feeling quite exceptionally merry.
> A stranger asked him: "Can you tell me, pray,
>   The quickest way to Brompton Cemetery?"
> "The quickest way? You bet I can!" said Gus,
>   And pushed the fellow underneath a bus.
>
> Whatever people say about my son,
> He does enjoy his little bit of fun.

13

Children are also often accused of being very blood-thirsty. Here is a poem by Ogden Nash on the subject – 'Don't Cry, Darling, It's Blood All Right':

Whenever poets want to give you the idea
　　that something is particularly meek and
　　mild,
They compare it to a child,
Thereby proving that though poets with
　　poetry may be rife,
They don't know the facts of life.
If of compassion you desire either a tittle or a
　　jot,
Don't try to get it from a tot.
Hard-boiled, sophisticated adults like me and
　　you
May enjoy ourselves thoroughly with 'Little
　　Women' and 'Winnie-the-Pooh',
But innocent infants these titles from their
　　reading course eliminate
As soon as they discover that it was honey
　　and nuts and mashed potatoes instead of
　　human flesh that Winnie-the-Pooh and
　　Little Women ate.
Innocent infants have no use for fables about
　　rabbits or donkeys or tortoises or porpoises,
What they want is something with plenty of
　　well-mutilated corpoises.
Not on legends of how the rose came to be a
　　rose instead of a petunia is their fancy fed,

But on the inside story of how somebody's
    bones got ground up to make somebody
    else's bread.
They'll go to sleep listening to the story of the
    little beggarmaid who got to be queen by
    being kind to the bees and birds,
But they're all eyes and ears the minute they
    suspect a wolf or a giant is going to tear
    some poor woodcutter into quarters or
    thirds.
It really doesn't take much to fill their cup;
All they want is for somebody to be eaten up.
Therefore I say unto you, all you poets who
    are so crazy about meek and mild little
    children and their angelic air,
If you are sincere and really want to please
    them, why just go out and get yourselves
    devoured by a bear.

To end this chapter on dislike of children, here are two quick thoughts, the first from Robert Benchley:

> In America there are two classes of travel –
> first class, and with children.

The other's much older. It was said by Democritus in the fifth century B.C.:

> I do not think that one should have children.

2

little angels

Children have always been loved – sometimes with unquestioning adoration, sometimes with a bit more commonsense. Lionel Kauffman:

> Children are a great comfort in your old age – and they help you reach it faster too.

Logan Pearsall Smith:

> What is more enchanting than the voices of young people when you can't hear what they say?

A definition by Ambrose Bierce of infancy:

> The period of our lives when, according to Wordsworth, 'Heaven lies about us.' The world begins lying about us pretty soon afterward.

Fran Lebowitz also noted their advantages:

> Children do not sit next to one in restaurants
> and discuss their preposterous hopes for the
> future in loud tones.

And a thought from Groucho Marx:

> My mother loved children – she would have
> given anything if I had been one.

Children have always been an inspiration to writers, but not all writers have always been very accurate about what children are really like. Poets, in particular, tend to get a bit carried away on the subject. William Canton:

> In praise of little children I will say
> God first made man, then found a better way
> For woman, but his third way was the best,
> Of all created things the loveliest
> And most divine are children.

And it's not just poets. Here's Mary Howitt, writing in the nineteenth century:

> God sends children for another purpose than
> merely to keep up the race – to enlarge our
> hearts, to make us unselfish, and full of
> kindly sympathies and affections; to give our
> souls higher aims, and to call out all our

faculties to extended enterprise and exertion;
to bring round our fireside bright faces and
happy smiles, and loving tender hearts. My
Soul blesses the Great Father every day, that
he has gladdened the earth with Little
Children.

Writers have always wanted to treat children as ideas –
ideas of innocence, ideas of hope, ideas of anything
except for real flesh-and-blood children. They also
enjoy imagining that children have miraculous powers of insight, that they can understand things
grown-ups find difficult. The kind of thing I mean is
expressed in this piece by George Gilfillan. He was a
nineteenth-century minister and critic, who was Scot-
tish and didn't have any children of his own:

Oh! how precious to me have been the
prattlings of little children, and those subtle
questions and those still subtler replies that I
have heard coming from their spotless lips,

19

and have listened to as to oracular breathings! How true the words, 'Out of the mouths of babes and sucklings thou hast ordained strength'; ay, strength of insight, to which that of most philosophers and theologians is abject weakness and folly. Almost every doctrine now 'most surely believed' by me, I have heard again . . . from the lips of prattlers ere or after their evening prayer was said, at the hour when . . ., as a double portion of the child's spirit seems to fall on them, their utterances sometimes far transcend the thoughts of the highest genius.

I think what children definitely can do is to see things very straight. Grown-ups get terribly involved in all the details of a subject, and often can't see the wood for trees. Children are more direct. A reminiscence by James Agate:

> A schoolgirl answered the question, 'In what countries are elephants found?' – 'Elephants are very large and intelligent animals and are seldom lost.'

There's a lot to be said for telling the truth. Here's an extract from Henry James's novel, *What Maisie Knew*:

> In the carriage, her mother, all kisses, ribbons, eyes, arms, strange sounds and sweet smells, said to her: 'And did your beastly papa, my precious angel, send any message to your

own loving mama?'

Then it was that she found the words
spoken by her beastly papa, to be, after all, in
her little bewildered ears, from which, at her
mother's appeal, they passed, in her clear
shrill voice, straight to her little innocent lips.

'He said I was to tell you, from him,' she
faithfully reported, 'that you're a nasty horrid
pig!'

Yes, if you're asked a question, it makes good sense to
answer it. Here's a modern fable by James Thurber,
called 'The Godfather and His Godchild':

21

A worldly-wise collector, who had trotted the globe collecting everything he could shoot, or buy, or make off with, called upon his godchild, a little girl of five, after a year of collecting in various countries of the world.

'I want to give you three things,' he said. 'Any three things your heart desires. I have diamonds from Africa, and a rhinoceros horn, scarabs from Egypt, emeralds from Guatemala, chessmen of ivory and gold, mooses' antlers, signal drums, ceremonial gongs, temple bells, and three rare and remarkable dolls. Now tell me,' he concluded, patting the little girl on the head, 'what do you want more than anything else in the world?'

His little godchild, who was not a hesitator, did not hesitate. 'I want to break your glasses and spit on your shoes,' she said.

As well as thinking that children had special insights, a lot of writers have been very impressed by the innocence of children. Just as many Puritans believed all children were born naturally evil, other thinkers thought they were born completely good. Here's John Earle, writing in 1623:

(A Child) is Nature's fresh picture newly drawn in oil, which time, and much handling, dims and defaces. His Soul is yet a white paper unscribbled with observations of the world, wherewith at length, it becomes a blurred notebook.

The English poet most hooked on the innocence of childhood was William Wordsworth. Constantly, through his work, he reverts to the same theme. He expresses his belief in his 'Ode on Intimations of Immortality':

Our birth is but a sleep and a forgetting:
    The Soul that rises with us, our Life's Star,
Hath somewhere else its setting,
    And cometh from afar;
Not in entire forgetfulness,
And not in utter nakedness,
But trailing clouds of glory do we come
    From God, who is our home:
Heaven lies about us in our infancy!
Shades of the prison-house begin to close
    Upon the growing boy,
But he beholds the light, and whence it flows,
    He sees it in his joy;
The youth, who daily farther from the east
    Must travel, still is Nature's priest,
    And by the vision splendid
    Is on his way attended;
At length the man perceives it die away,
And fade into the light of common day.

Well, if you couldn't make head or tail of all that, what Wordsworth was basically saying was that life starts perfect at birth, and thereafter gets progressively worse. Which is a rather depressing view.

Parents are notoriously blinkered about their own children. They see them as the most wonderful that ever existed. The German poet, Goethe:

23

> If children grew up according to early
> indications, we should have nothing but
> geniuses.

Parents are often the worst judges of their own children's abilities. Very few can be sensible about them; either they think their offspring are useless or brilliant. Usually this doesn't matter, because it's just a private opinion, but when the child in question is actually a performer, it can become more difficult. There have always been child stars. Charles Dickens created one in *Nicholas Nickleby*. Nicholas joins up with the touring theatrical troupe of Mr Vincent Crummles and is introduced to Mr Crummles's daughter:

> There bounded on to the stage, from some
> mysterious inlet, a little girl in a dirty white
> frock with tucks up to the knees, short
> trousers, sandalled shoes, white spencer, pink
> gauze bonnet, green veil, and curl papers;
> who turned a pirouette, cut twice in the air,
> turned another pirouette, then, looking off at
> the opposite wing, shrieked, bounded forward
> to within six inches of the footlights, and fell
> into a beautiful attitude of terror, as a shabby
> gentleman in an old pair of buff slippers came
> in at one powerful slide, and, chattering his
> teeth, fiercely brandished a walking stick.
>   'They are going through "The Indian
> Savage and the Maiden," ' said Mrs.
> Crummles.

24

The Indian Savage and the Maiden turns out to be a ballet of quite unbelievable awfulness, but at the end of it Mr Crummles is hugely enthusiastic:

'Very well indeed,' said Mr. Crummles; 'bravo!'

'Bravo!' cried Nicholas, resolved to make the best of everything. 'Beautiful!'

'This, sir,' said Mr. Vincent Crummles, bringing the maiden forward, 'this is the infant phenomenon – Miss Ninetta Crummles.'

'Your daughter?' inquired Nicholas.

'My daughter – my daughter,' replied Mr. Vincent Crummles; 'the idol of every place we go into sir. We have had complimentary letters about this girl, sir, from the nobility and gentry of almost every town in England.'

'I am not surprised at that,' said Nicholas; 'she must be quite a natural genius.'

'Quite a . . .!' Mr. Crummles stopped; language was not powerful enough to describe the infant phenomenon. 'I'll tell you what, sir,' he said, 'the talent of this child is not to be imagined. She must be seen, sir – seen – to be ever so faintly appreciated. There; go to your mother, my dear.'

'May I ask how old she is?' inquired Nicholas.

'You may, sir,' replied Mr. Crummles, looking steadily in his questioner's face, as some men do when they have doubts about being implicitly believed in what they are going to say. 'She is ten years of age, sir.'

'Not more!'

'Not a day.'

'Dear me!' said Nicholas, 'it's extraordinary.'

It was; for the infant phenomenon, though of short stature, had a comparatively aged countenance; and had, moreover, been precisely the same age – not, perhaps, to the full extent of the memory of the oldest inhabitant, but certainly for five good years. But she had been kept up late every night, and put upon an unlimited allowance of gin-and-water from infancy, to prevent her growing tall; and perhaps this system of training had produced in the infant phenomenon these additional phenomena.

Some parents are all too ready to see their children as prodigies. And, after all, what is a prodigy? Here's a definition by J. B. Morton:

PRODIGY – A child who plays the piano when he ought to be asleep in bed.

Few parents think their children are prodigies, but that doesn't prevent them from being fond of their offspring and from being upset when they leave home. A child's departure for boarding school can be a traumatic time for the parents. In Geoffrey Willans

and Ronald Searle's book *How To Be Topp*, the awful
schoolboy, Nigel Molesworth, shows the change of
relationship in a series of letters written from school to
home. The first is the 'new bug's' letter:

                              st. custard's,
Darling mama, darling papa,
     i mis you very much. i am lonly. plees kiss
my gollywog. never did I apreciate so much
the joys and comforts of home life. To think
that i was rud to grandad that i scremed when

i was told to hav a bath. And how many
times hav i refused to come in and go to bed.
O woe. Kiss my gollywog agane.
Yours fathefuly
binkie.
nb you had beter kiss grandad too. Or not. As
you plese.

But it only takes a few weeks of school for the letters to
become rather shorter and less emotional:

LETER: st. custard's
Sunda.
Dearest Mummy (and Daddy)
　We played aganst porridge court on
saturday. We lost 9-0. The film was a western.
Will you send me a bakterial gun. They are
6/6 at grabbers.
With love from
Nigel.

ANSER:
Barleywaters.
Clotshire.
Monda
My dearest darling most beloved nigel,
　It was marvelous super to get your lovely
long leter with all its news. I have telephoned
grabbers to send the gun. *Are you taking your
lozenges?* Please let me kno. Wot a shame
about porridge court i xpect you will win next

28

year. There is very litle to tell you. the snodrops are out and yore father is in a filthy temper but these facts hav nothing to do with each other. Do not forget, darling, to let me kno about the lozenges

Your fondest superest ever-loving

Mummy.

P.S. *Don't* forget about the lozenges, darling.

LETER:

st. custard's.

Sunda.

Dear Mummy and Daddy,

We played aganst howler house on Saturday. We lost 9-0. The film was micky mouse. Thank you for the bakterial gun. Will you send me a jet-propeled airship. (17/6)

Love from

nigel.

ANSER:

Barleywaters, Clotshire.

My ever-darlingest superest most smashing and admired son Nigel,

Your letter was a wonderful surprise and so full of news. Your handriting hav improved beyond mesure. *You did not mention about the lozenges darling will you be sure and let me kno next time.* Do not wory too much about your lessons i kno you are doing your best. The crocus are out now but yore father is still in a

filthy temper so i hav ordered the jet-propeled
airship myself. Don't forget about the
lozenges and Gollywog send his love.
    Your most tremendously affectionate
divinely superly adoring mater

                              Mummy
p.s don't forget about the lozenges.

One thing that Nigel Molesworth isn't is a little goody
goody, but there are plenty of those in English literature. Interestingly, a lot of them were called 'little'.

Goody Two-Shoes's real name was Little Margery.
Dickens created Little Nell and Little Dorrit. Harriet
Beecher Stowe created Little Eva in *Uncle Tom's Cabin*.
And then of course there was Little Lord Fauntleroy,
who was brought to life by Frances Hodgson Burnett. I
mean, we all know children can be jolly nice, but I
think this is taking it a bit far. . .:

Every month of his life he grew handsomer and more interesting.

When he was old enough to walk out with his nurse, dragging a small wagon and wearing a short white kilt skirt, and a big white hat set back on his curly yellow hair, he was so handsome and strong and rosy that he attracted everyone's attention, and his nurse would come home and tell his mama stories of the ladies who had stopped their carriages to look at and speak to him, and of how pleased they were when he talked to them in his cheerful little way, as if he had known them always. His greatest charm was this cheerful, fearless, quaint little way of making friends with people. I think it arose from his having a very confiding nature, and a kind little heart that sympathised with everyone, and wished to make everyone as comfortable as he wished to be himself.

At least when Hilaire Belloc tackled the subject of goodness, he showed a sense of humour about it. Here's his poem about 'Charles Augustus Fortescue, Who Always Did what was Right, and so accumulated an Immense Fortune':

The nicest child I ever knew
Was Charles Augustus Fortescue.
He never lost his cap or tore
His stockings or his pinafore:

31

In eating Bread he made no crumbs,
He was extremely fond of Sums,
To which, however, he preferred
The Parsing of a Latin Word –
He sought, when it was in his power,
For information, twice an hour,
And as for finding mutton-fat
Unappetising, far from that!
He often, at his Father's Board,
Would beg them, of his own accord,
To give him, if they did not mind,
The greasiest morsels they could find –
His later years did not belie
The Promise of his Infancy.
In Public Life he always tried
To take a judgement Broad and Wide;
In private none was more than he
Renowned for quiet courtesy.
He rose at once in his career,
And long before his fortieth year
Had wedded Fifi, Only Child
Of Bunyan, First Lord Aberfylde.
He thus became Immensely Rich,
And built the splendid mansion which
Is called "The Cedars, Muswell Hill",
Where he resides in Affluence still
To show what everybody might
Become by
        SIMPLY DOING RIGHT.

The idea of goody-goody literature is that the child reading it should immediately imitate the example of the perfect child in the book. But most independent children are more likely to react by doing the exact opposite. Charlotte Brontë's Jane Eyre was a very independent child. Here she is being questioned by the pious Mr Brocklehurst:

'Do you say your prayers night and morning?' continued my interrogator.
'Yes, sir.'
'Do you read your Bible?'
'Sometimes.'
'With pleasure? Are you fond of it?'
'I like Revelations, and the book of Daniel, and Genesis and Samuel, and a little bit of Exodus, and some parts of Kings and Chronicles, and Job and Jonah.'
'And the Psalms? I hope you like them?'
'No, sir.'
'No? oh, shocking! I have a little boy, younger than you, who knows six Psalms by heart: and when you ask him which he would rather have, a ginger-bread nut to eat, or a verse of a Psalm to learn, he says: "Oh! the verse of a Psalm! angels sing Psalms;" says he, "I wish to be a little angel here below;" he then gets two nuts in recompense for his infant piety.'
'Psalms are not interesting,' I remarked.
'That proves you have a wicked heart; and

you must pray to God to change it: to give
you a new and clean one: to take away your
heart of stone and give you a heart of flesh.'

The trouble is that good children of the past come
across to modern readers as insufferable prigs. If one
looks at Dean Farrar's famous book *Eric; or, Little by
Little*, it is hard to imagine that the people who read it
when it first came out in 1858 took it seriously. But
they did:

One day as the two were walking together in
the green playground, Mr. Gordon passed by;
and as the boys touched their caps, he
nodded and smiled pleasantly at Russell, but
hardly noticed, and did not return Eric's

salute. He had begun to dislike the latter more and more, and had given him up altogether as one of the reprobates. . . .

'What a surly devil that is,' said Eric, when he had passed; 'did you see how he purposely cut me?'

'A surly . . .? Oh, Eric, that's the first time I ever heard you swear.'

Eric blushed.

Children's stories, particularly those of a slightly whimsical type have not always been universally popular. And they are very easy to send up. Alan Coren wondered what had become of one childhood favourite:

Winnie-the-Pooh is sixty now, but looks far older. His eyes dangle, and he suffers from terminal moth. He walks into things a lot. I asked him about that, as we sat in the pitiful dinginess which had surrounded him for almost half a century.

'Punchy,' said Winnie-the-Pooh, 'is what I am. I've been to some of the best people, Hamley's, Mothercare, they all say the same thing: there's nothing you can do about it, it's all that hammering you took in the old days.'

Bitterly, he flicked open a well-thumbed copy of *Winnie-the-Pooh*, and read the opening lines aloud:

'"Here is Edward Bear, coming downstairs now, bump, bump, bump, on the back of his head, behind Christopher Robin. It is, as far as he knows, the only way of coming downstairs."'

He looked at me. . . . 'You think I didn't want to walk down, like normal people? But what chance did I stand? Every morning, it was the same story, this brat comes in and grabs me and next thing I know the old skull is bouncing on the lousy lino. Also,' he barked a short bitter laugh, 'that was the last time anyone called me Edward Bear. A distinguished name, Edward. A name with class. After the King, you know.'

I nodded. 'I know,' I said.

'But did it suit the Milnes?' Pooh hurled the book into the grate, savagely. 'Did it suit the itsy-bitsy, mumsy-wumsy, ooze-daddy's-ickle-boy-den Milnes? So I was Winnie-the-Pooh. You want to know what it was like when the Milnes hit the sack and I got chucked in the toy cupboard for the night?'

'What?' I said.

'It was "Hello, sailor!" and "Give us a kiss, Winifred!" and "Watch out, Golly, I think he fancies you!" not to mention,' and here he clenched his sad, mangy little fists, 'the standard "Oy, anyone else notice there's a peculiar poo in here, ha, ha, ha!"'

J. B. Morton had a go at another part of A. A. Milne's output. Here are a couple of verses from his proposed book, *When We Were Very Silly*. The first one's called 'Theobald James':

I've got a silk-worm,
A teeny-tiny silk-worm;
I call *my* silk-worm
Theobald James.
But nursie says it's cruel,
Nursie says it's wicked
To call a teeny-tiny little
  Silk-
  Worm
  NAMES.

I said to *my* silk-worm
  'Oh, Mr. Silk-worm,
I'd rather be a silk-worm
Than anything, far!'
And nursie says he answered,
Nursie says he shouted,
'You wish you were a silk-worm?
You little
  Prig,
  You
  ARE!'

The second's called 'Now We Are Sick':

Hush, hush,
Nobody cares!
Christopher Robin
Has
  Fallen
    Down-
      Stairs.

Rotten, really, isn't it, to make fun of books that have
given so much pleasure to so many children. But if the
books are really good, they can take it. Anyway, some
don't need to be made fun of; they do it for themselves. Here's a bit from one of the great goody-goody
books of all time, *Pollyanna* by Eleanor H. Porter. The
book was written in 1913 and was so widely read that
nowadays a Pollyanna has come to mean someone
who always looks on the bright side. However black
the clouds above her, eleven-year-old Pollyanna can
always see the silver lining by playing the 'just being
glad' game. Here's how she and her father first did it
(described to the maid Nancy):

'Why, we began it on some crutches that
came in a missionary barrel.'
  '*Crutches!*'
  'Yes. You see, I'd wanted a doll, and Father
had written them so; but when the barrel
came the lady wrote that there hadn't any
dolls come in, but the little crutches had. So

she sent 'em along as they might come in
handy for some child, some time. And that's
when we began it.'

'Well, I must say I can't see any game about
that,' declared Nancy, almost irritably.

'Oh, yes; the game was to just find
something about everything to be glad about –
no matter what 'twas,' rejoined Pollyanna
earnestly. 'And we began right then – on the
crutches.'

'Well, goodness me! I can't see anythin' ter
be glad about – gettin' a pair of crutches when
you wanted a doll!'

Pollyanna clapped her hands.

39

'There is – there is,' she crowed. 'But *I* couldn't see it, either, Nancy, at first,' she added, with quick honesty. 'Father had to tell it to me.'

'Well, then, suppose *you* tell *me*,' almost snapped Nancy.

'Goosey! Why, just be glad because you *don't–need-'em*!' exulted Pollyanna triumphantly.

Aren't children wonderful? I'll finish the chapter with an observation from P. G. Wodehouse's Bertie Wooster:

I don't know why it is, but I've never been able to bear with fortitude anything in the shape of a kid with golden curls. Confronted with one, I feel the urge to step on him or drop things on him from a height.

3

school

Everyone's had some form of education, but not everyone enjoys school, or respects it. The dancer, Isadora Duncan:

> It seems to me that the general education a child receives at school is absolutely useless.

Oscar Wilde:

> Education is an admirable thing, but it is well to remember from time to time that nothing worth knowing can be taught.

Gwen Raverat:

> The chief thing I learnt at school was how to tell lies.

We all start learning, really, as soon as we are born,

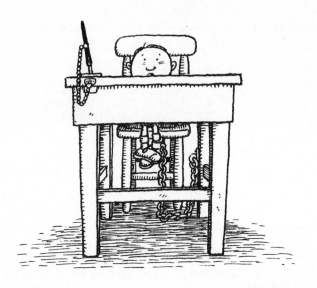

and go on learning right through our lives. We do some of our learning in school, but we also learn from looking at the world around us, talking to people, reading books, watching television, playing games – everything teaches. So does it matter what children are taught first? Dr Johnson was once asked that question, and this was his reply:

Sir, it is no matter what you teach them first any more than what leg you shall put into your breeches first. Sir, you may stand disputing which is best to put in first, but in the mean time your breech is bare. Sir, while you are considering which of two things you should teach your child first, another boy has learnt them both.

42

In the past, a lot of children's education consisted of learning things by heart. This was partly because school books were expensive and comparatively rare, but more because it was thought to be a good way of training a young mind. And who knows, maybe it is. John Ruskin, writing in *Praeterita*, reckoned it worked for him:

> Walter Scott and Pope's Homer were reading
> of my own election, and my mother forced
> me, by steady daily toil, to learn long chapters
> of the Bible by heart; as well as to read it
> every syllable through, aloud, hard names
> and all, from Genesis to the Apocalypse,
> about once a year: and to that discipline –
> patient, accurate, and resolute – I owe, not
> only a knowledge of the book, which I find
> occasionally serviceable, but much of my
> general power of taking pains, and the best
> part of my taste in literature.

It wasn't just in posh families that learning the Bible was so much part of education. When he was writing his *Tour Through the Whole Island of Great Britain*, in the early part of the eighteenth century, Daniel Defoe visited a village school in Somerset:

> I observed one of the lowest scholars was reading his lesson to the usher, which lesson it seems was a chapter in the Bible, so I sat down by the master, till the boy had read out his chapter. I observed the boy read a little oddly in the tone of the country, which made me the more attentive, because on enquiry, I found that the words were the same, and the orthography the same as in all our Bibles. I observed also the boy read it out with his eyes still on the book, and his head like a mere boy, moving from side to side, as the lines reached cross the columns of the book; his lesson was in the (Song of Solomon) Chapter 5, Verse 3, or which the words are these:
>> 'I have washed my coat, how shall I put it on,
>> I have washed my feet, how shall I defile them?'
>
> The boy read thus, with his eyes, as I say, full on the text.
>> 'Chava doffed my cooat, how shall I don't, chava washed my veet, how shall I moil 'em?'
>
> How the dexterous dunce could form his mouth to express so readily the words, (which

stood right printed in the book) in his country jargon, I could not but admire.

This emphasis on learning great chunks of books by heart obviously had a great effect on children's education. It also produced some very advanced children, who seemed to have read and learnt everything they could lay their hands on. Here is the seventeenth-century diarist, John Evelyn, talking about his son Richard, who died aged five years and three days:

At two yeares and halfe old he could perfectly reade any of the English, Latine, French, or Gottic letters, pronouncing the three first languages exactly. He had before the fifth yeare, or in that yeare, not onely skill to reade most written hands, but to decline all the nouns, conjugate the verbs regular, and most of the irregular... The number of verses he could recite was prodigious, and what he remembered of the parts of playes; which he would also act; and when seeing a Plautus in one's hand, he ask'd what book it was, and being told it was comedy, and too difficult for him, he wept for sorrow. Strange was his apt and ingenious application of fables and morals, for he had read Aesop; he had a wonderful disposition to mathematics, having by heart divers propositions of Euclid that were read to him in play, and he would make lines and demonstrate them.

Another prodigy, who lived some hundred and fifty years after Evelyn's son, was Thomas Babington – later Lord – Macaulay. At the age of four, he had some hot coffee spilt on him (I think the temptation to spill hot coffee on a child of that sort must have been strong) and, after an interval, when his hostess asked if it still hurt, he replied:

46

Thank you, madam, the agony is abated.

There have always been prodigies, just as there have always been children with photographic memories. That sort of instant recall can have surprising effects, as this reminiscence of John Aubrey shows. He is talking about the schooldays of the lawyer, John Hoskyns:

> He was of a strong constitution, and had a prodigious memorie. I remember I have heard that one time he had not made his exercise (verse) and spake to one of his Forme to shew him his, which he sawe. The Schoolmaster presently calles for the Exercises, and Hoskyns told him that he had writ it out but lost it, but could repeat it, and repeated the other boye's exercise (I think 12 or 16 verses) only at once reading over. When the boy who really had made them shewed the Master the same, and could not repeat them, he was whipped for stealing Hoskyns' exercise.

Unfair, unfair. It's funny how quickly one goes back to that schoolboy feeling of injustice. Memories of school remain very vivid right through life. Samuel Butler:

> I once heard two elderly men comparing notes about the way in which they still sometimes dreamed they were being bullied by their schoolmaster.

It doesn't take much to bring it all back. Some grown men say they can still remember the feelings they had on their first day at school. Laurie Lee recalls starting at a Gloucestershire country school in *Cider With Rosie*:

I spent that first day picking holes in paper,
then went home in a smouldering temper.
  'What's the matter, Loll? Didn't he like
school, then?'
  'They never gave me the present.'
  'Present? What present?'
  'They said they'd give me a present.'
  'Well, now, I'm sure they didn't.'
  'They did! They said: "You're Laurie Lee,
ain't you? Well, you just sit there for the
present." I sat there all day but I never got it.
I ain't going back there again!'

But he, like everyone else, did have to go back. Day after day. Perhaps the things that give most feeling of the continuity of schools, of all the pupils who've been through them, sitting in exactly the same places, are the scribbles they left – their carvings on desks or their doodlings in text-books. In the last century school-boys started writing little rhymes in their books to deter thieves. Here are a couple:

Black is the raven
Black is the rook
But Blacker the Sinner
That pinches this book.

This book is mine
This boot another
Touch not the one
For fear of the other.

Schools used to be pretty tough places to grow up in.
A lot of them prided themselves on the rigorous lives
their pupils lived, eating dull food and working long
hours. John Aubrey didn't approve of this. Here's his
recommendation:

No scholar to rise too early (especially in
Winter), because it checks their perspiration
and so, dulls them; and it stints their growth.
Some friends of mine impute their
unluckiness to their too early rising at
Westminster.

Oliver Goldsmith, writing a century later, was no
keener on the Spartan approach to schooling:

How very wrong those parents are, who
attempt to improve the health and strength of
their children by too hardy an education; and
though some may survive such attempts, they
seem insensible how many die under the
experiment. Peter the Great, in order to teach
some children to be perfect sailors, instituted,
that they should be permitted to drink only
sea-water; their instructors obeyed the order,
but all the children died.

As well as the hardships imposed by their living conditions, schoolchildren used also to suffer a great deal from their teachers. It's difficult for us nowadays to imagine how closely linked the ideas of education and beating used to be. For a long time it was thought that flogging was not only a useful punishment, but also a necessary step to learning. Here's an old nursery rhyme:

Doctor Faustus was a good man,
He whipped his scholars now and then;
When he whipped them he made them dance,
Out of England into France,
Out of France into Spain,
And then he whipped them back again!

And he was a good man. The idea of the necessity of flogging was deep-rooted. From the Bible:

He that spareth his rod hateth his son.

An old proverb:

Gold must be beaten, and a child scourged.

In 'Don Juan' Lord Byron took it for granted:

O ye who teach the ingenuous youth of
    nations –
  Holland, France, England, Germany or
    Spain;
I pray ye flog them upon all occasions,
  It mends their morals – never mind the
    pain.

There were always a few enlightened souls, who saw the pointlessness of trying to beat knowledge into children, but they were definitely in the minority. John Aubrey was against flogging, though for 'serious naughtiness' among his pupils he recommended the use of thumb-screws. And Richard Steele had this to say on the subject in 1711:

I am confident that no Boy who will not be allured to Letters without Blows, will ever be brought to anything with them. A great or good Mind must necessarily be the worse for such Indignities: and it is a sad Change to lose of its Virtue for the Improvement of its Knowledge.

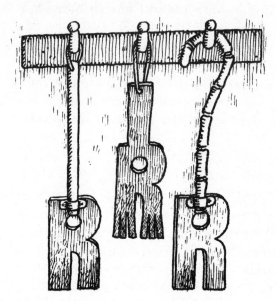

But unfortunately such voices of good sense were rare and for a long time the two ideas of a schoolmaster and a cane were inseparable. They certainly were in Frank Richard's Billy Bunter books, where the Fat Owl of the Remove was constantly getting on the wrong side of his form-master, Mr Quelch. Here's an extract from *Bunter Does His Best!*:

> 'I shall cane you –.'
> 'Oh, lor'!'
> '– severely –!'

'Ow!'

Mr. Quelch picked up a cane from his table. Billy Bunter watched that proceeding with the deepest apprehension. The Remove master pointed to a chair with the cane.

'Bunter! Bend over that chair!'

'Oh, crikey!'

'At once!' thundered Mr. Quelch.

In the lowest possible spirits, Billy Bunter bent over the chair. The cane swished and descended. Billy Bunter's tight trousers fairly rang under the swipe.

'Wow!' roared Bunter.

Swipe!

'Yow!'

Swipe!

'Yarooooh!'

Billy Bunter had been 'whopped' before: often, though not so often as he had deserved. But he had never had it like this before! Quelch was putting his beef into it. Apparently he thought it his duty to be severe in this flagrant case: and Quelch was a whale on duty. He was running no risk of spoiling Bunter by sparing the rod! Swipe!

'Yow-ow-ow-ow-ow!'

Swipe!

'Yooo-hooooooop!'

Swipe!

It was six of the best – the very best! . . . The final swipe of the six evoked a roar that

must have awakened most of the echoes in
Masters' Studies.

'Now, Bunter –.'

'Yow-ow-ow-ow!'

'Let that be a warning to you, Bunter –.'

'Wow! wow! wow!'

'Cease those ridiculous noises at once,
Bunter –.'

'Ooooooooooooooooooooh!'

'Ow-ow-ow-wow-wow-wow!'

A mumbling Fat Owl rolled out of the
study, and wriggled away down the passage
like a fat eel. Sounds of woe floated back as
Bunter departed.

But the marks of the cane are not the only impressions
left by schoolteachers. Here's an extract from Samuel
Butler's book *The Way of All Flesh*, which follows a
savage portrait of a headmaster:

O schoolmasters – if any of you read this book
– bear in mind when any particularly timid
drivelling urchin is brought by his papa into
your study, and you treat him with the
contempt which he deserves, and afterwards
make his life a burden to him for years – bear
in mind that it is exactly in the disguise of
such a boy as this that your future chronicler
will appear. Never see a wretched little
heavy-eyed mite sitting on the edge of a chair
against your study wall without saying to

yourselves, 'perhaps this boy is he who, if I am not careful, will one day tell the world what manner of man I was.' If even two or three schoolmasters learn this lesson and remember it, the preceding chapters will not have been written in vain.

Not all writers describe schoolteachers with such viciousness. Sometimes one senses a lot of affection for the breed. Here's a charming description of a schoolmistress by Henry James:

> (She was) a stout red-faced lady with grey hair and a large apron, the latter convenience somehow suggesting, as she stood about with a resolute air, that she viewed her little pupils as so many small slices cut from the loaf of life and on which she was to dab the butter of arithmetic and spelling, accompanied by way of jam with a light application of the practice of prize-giving.

Probably one of the most enduring fictional schoolteachers is the awful Mr Wackford Squeers, who rules over Dotheboys Hall in Charles Dickens's *Nicholas Nickleby*. Nicholas gets a job as assistant master at Dotheboys and is introduced to the school's novel educational method by Mr Squeers:

> 'This is the first class in English spelling and philosophy, Nickleby,' said Squeers,

beckoning Nicholas to stand beside him.
'We'll get up a Latin one, and hand that over
to you. Now, then, where's the first boy?'

'Please, sir, he's cleaning the back parlour
window,' said the temporary head of the
philosophical class.

'So he is, to be sure,' rejoined Squeers. 'We
go upon the practical mode of teaching,
Nickleby; the regular education system.
C-l-e-a-n, clean, verb active, to make bright,
to scour. W-i-n, win, d-e-r, der, winder, a
casement. When the boy knows this out of
book, he goes and does it.'

The trouble was that, in days when most children
worked for their living, education wasn't thought that
important. Here's further evidence of this, from a
school log book, quoted in Ronald Blythe's book,
Akenfield:

1886 – The children won't come to school.
Only one out of the above list (of twelve
names) attended this week. Such irregularity
is very disheartening.
1889 – There is now a Night School for the
children who must work in the day-time.

Attendance bad. Picking stones has ended
and weeding in the fields still continues. The
school has been open 30 times this month and
Frederick Walls has attended half a day.
Twenty boys hardly ever attend and are seen
working.

Nowadays the laws are tighter and, though there is still quite a bit of truancy, it's more difficult to avoid school. And to avoid all the things that go with school. Like exams, for instance. One way or another, under one name or another, they seem to crop up in most school systems. But be encouraged – they aren't infallible tests of brightness. Oscar Wilde:

> In examinations the foolish ask questions that the wise cannot answer.

And, anyway, a lot of people have done very well in life without excelling at exams. Here's how Sir Winston Churchill approached his entrance to Harrow:

> I wrote my name at the top of the page. I wrote down the number of the question '1'. After much reflection, I put a bracket round it thus '(1)'. But thereafter I could not think of anything connected with it that was either relevant or true. . . It was from these slender indications of scholarship that Mr. Weldon drew the conclusion that I was worthy to pass into Harrow. It is very much to his credit.

Perhaps, while we're on the subject, we ought to have a brief examination paper. Here's one written by Sellar and Yeatman, the authors of *1066 And All That*. It comes from their follow-up book, *And Now All This*:

TEST PAPER
ON
ABSOLUTELY GENERAL KNOWLEDGE
Time allowed – 5 Minutes

1. How are you?
2. *Who* are you?
3. *Who gave you that name?*
4. (a) Can you give us the right time? Or
   (b) Are you a stranger in these parts
      yourself?
   (N.B. Candidates marked with an asterisk
   may use the india-rubber.)

59

5. What are you doing now?
6. (i) What would you like to do next?
   (ii) Have you done it?
   (iii) What are you thinking about now?
7. 'Father & Mother had I none, but that man's father was my father's fag at Oxford.' *What do you know about that!*
8. (a) If there were ten horses in for a race and you burned your boots and put your shirt on the favourite and said you would eat your hat if it didn't come in first and it came in last and they couldn't get the shirt off and you'd left your hat in the cloak-room... (b) Are you attending?
9. Would you like to stop now? (If so, (i) hand in your paper if you have written anything on it, and (ii) tear up your blotting-paper if you have drawn anything silly on it.)
10. *(a) Have you got nice physical features? If so,
   (b) Are you doing anything this evening?
   *For women candidates only.

I think I'll finish this chapter on school by having a little pity for teachers. Theirs is a hard lot. More wisdom from Sellar and Yeatman:

For every person wishing to teach there are thirty not wishing to be taught.

60

4
play

Almost all children like playing, and so do a surprising number of adults. But not all. Oscar Wilde:

Football is all very well as a game for rough girls, but it is hardly suitable for delicate boys.

Fran Lebowitz:

> Children make the most desirable opponents
> in Scrabble as they are both easy to beat and
> fun to cheat.

Dr Laurence J. Peter:

> Give a child enough rope and he will trip you
> up.

Playing is an important activity, and time spent in
playing is rarely wasted. In the words of Montaigne:

> It is to be noted that children's plays are not
> sports, and should be regarded as their most
> serious actions.

Play is also necessary for children to break the mono-
tony of school. Here's an extract from *Greyling Towers*,
a girls' story written by Mrs Molesworth:

> 'It isn't only about today being rainy that I
> mind,' the elder little sister went on. 'It's all
> our life! I do think it is dull. One day after
> another much the same. Breakfast, dinner and
> tea – history, jography, French, writing, sums;
> going to bed and getting up, and then all
> beginning again just the same.'
> 'There's dancing twice a week,' said Viva,
> rather timidly . . . 'and there's holidays
> sometimes.'

62

Some children play very happily on their own, but for most it's more fun when they've got someone else to play with. A rather sad reminiscence from John Aubrey:

'Twas a great disadvantage to me in my childhood . . . to be bred up in a kind of Parke far from Neighbours and no Child to converse withall: so that I did not speake till late. My father had one to teach me in the house, and I was pent-up in a Roome by my selfe melancholy.

But you can't just play with *anybody*. Here's a description of unsuccessful play from Jane Austen's *Mansfield Park*:

The holiday allowed to the Miss Bertrams the next day, on purpose to afford leisure for getting acquainted with, and entertaining their young cousin, produced little union. They could not but hold her cheap on finding that she had but two sashes, and had never learnt French; and when they perceived her to be little struck with the duet they were so good as to play, they could do no more than make her a generous present of some of their least valued toys, and leave her to herself while they adjourned to whatever might be the favourite holiday sport of the moment, making artificial flowers or wasting gold paper.

And even if the company is right, there are other
threats to successful play. Parents can get in the way.
In Victorian times parents were very strict about what
was and wasn't allowed. Here's a snippet from
Samuel Butler's *The Way of all Flesh*:

I was there on a Sunday, and observed the
rigour with which the young people were
taught to observe the Sabbath; they might not
cut out things, nor use their paint-box on a
Sunday, and this they thought rather hard,
because their cousins . . . might do these

64

things. Their cousins might play with their toy train on Sunday, but though they had promised that they would run none but Sunday trains, all traffic had been prohibited. One treat only was allowed them – on Sunday evenings they might choose their own hymns.

And if that sounds discouraging, how about this? In Charles Dickens's *Great Expectations* the hero Pip is sent to play at Miss Havisham's cobweb-laden house:

'Do you know what I touch here?' she said, laying her hands, one upon the other, on her left side.
'Yes, ma'am . . .'
'What do I touch?'
'Your heart?'
'Broken!'
She uttered the word with an eager look, and with strong emphasis, and with a weird smile that had a kind of boast in it. Afterwards, she kept her hands there for a little while, and slowly took them away as if they were heavy.
'I am tired,' said Miss Havisham. 'I want diversion, and I have done with men and women. Play.'
I think it will be conceded by my most disputatious reader that she could hardly have directed an unfortunate boy to do anything in the wide world more difficult to be done under the circumstances.

'I sometimes have sick fancies,' she went
on, 'and I have a sick fancy that I want to see
some play. There, there!' with an impatient
movement of the fingers of her right hand;
'play, play, play!'

Most children play under more congenial circumstances, and most start with cuddly toys and dolls.
Dolls have the advantage that they can take on any
identity or emotions that their owner wishes. Here's
the view of Sara Crewe, from Frances Hodgson
Burnett's story *A Little Princess*:

'What I believe about dolls,' she said, 'is that
they can do things they will not let us know
about. Perhaps, really, Emily can read and
talk and walk, but she will only do it when
people are out of the room. That is her secret.
You see, if people knew that dolls could do
things, they would make them work. So,
perhaps, they have promised each other to
keep it a secret. If you stay in the room, Emily
will just sit there and stare; but if you go out
she will begin to read, perhaps, or go and
look out of the window. Then, if she heard
either of us coming, she would just run back
and jump into her chair and pretend she had
been there all the time.'

A look around department stores at Christmas time
suggests that modern children are embarrassed by

66

choice of toys. But this was not always the case, particularly in a family that despised materialism. John Ruskin recalls his childhood in the 1820s:

Nor did I painfully wish, what I was never permitted for an instant to hope, or even imagine, the possession of such things as one saw in toy-shops. I had a bunch of keys to play with, as long as I was capable of pleasure in what glittered or jingled; as I grew older I had a cart, and a ball; and when I was five or six years old, two boxes of well-cut wooden bricks. With these modest, but, I still think, entirely sufficient possessions, and being always summarily whipped if I cried, did not

do as I was bid, or tumbled on the stairs, I
soon attained serene and secure methods of
life and motion; and could pass my days
contentedly tracing the squares and
comparing the colours of my carpet;
examining the knots in the wood of the floor,
or counting the bricks in the opposite houses.

But toys are not essential to play. The best games have
always been improvised from whatever is to hand. In
his memoirs James Stephen remembered growing up
in 1768:

I can recall the happiness that I experienced
... from catching the large yellow cucumbers
that floated from the gardener's grounds
down the creek towards Vauxhall, scooping
them into boats and rigging them with a
wooden rudder and a paper sail... I can
remember even preserving the fallen leaves of
Autumn, sticking them on broken panes of
glass to observe better their variegated tints
and fibres.

The beauties of nature have always offered oppor-
tunities for play, particularly for children brought up
in the country. The poet John Clare describes his
childhood at the end of the eighteenth century:

I grew so much into the quiet love of Nature's
preserves that I was never easy but when I

was in the fields, passing my sabbaths and leisure with the shepherds and herdboys as fancys prompted – sometimes playing at marbles on the smooth-beaten sheeptracks, or leapfrog among the thymy molehills, sometimes running among the corn to get the red and blue flowers for cockades to play at soldiers, or running into the woods to hunt strawberries, or stealing peas in churchtime, when the owners were safe, to boil at the gypseys' fire, who went half-shares at our stolen luxury.

Outdoor games seem to reach their peak of excitement when there is snow on the ground. Apart from the pleasures of making things with the sudden supply of freezing plasticine, whole new areas of winter sports are opened up. Tobogganing, and of course skating. William Wordsworth recalled the excitement of skating on a frozen lake in 'The Prelude':

> And in the frosty season, when the sun
> Was set, and visible for many a mile
> The cottage windows through the twilight
>   blazed,
> I heeded not the summons: happy time
> It was indeed for all of us – to me
> It was a time of rapture! Clear and loud
> The village clock tolled six, – I wheeled about
> Proud and exulting like an untired horse
> That cares not for its home. All shod with
>   steel

We hissed along the polished ice in games
Confederate, imitative of the chase
And woodland pleasures, – the resounding
   horn,
The loud pack bellowing, and the hunted hare.
So through the darkness and the cold we flew,
And not a voice was idle; with the din
Meanwhile, the precipices rang aloud;
The leafless tree and every icy crag
Tinkled like iron; while the distant hills
Into the tumult sent an alien sound
Of melancholy not unnoticed, while the stars
Eastward were sparkling clear, and in the
   west
The orange sky of evening died away.

Outdoor types will follow outdoor pursuits wherever they are. Here's Lord Baden-Powell's recollection of his school days at Charterhouse when he used to play in the woods outside the school walls:

> As a trapper I set my snares, and when I caught a rabbit or hare (which wasn't often) I learned by painful experiment to skin, clean and cook him. But knowing that the redskins were about, in the shape of masters looking for boys out of bounds, I used a very small non-smoky fire for fear of giving away my whereabouts.
>
> Incidentally, also, I gained sufficient cunning to hide up in trees when danger of this kind threatened, since experience told me that masters hunting for boys seldom looked upward.

Climbing trees has always been a popular childhood pastime. Bertrand Russell admitted that he used to do it:

> I had another amusement which I much enjoyed. On a Sunday, when the Park was crowded, I would climb to the very top of a large beech tree on the edge of our grounds. There I would hang upside down and scream and watch the crowd gravely discussing how a rescue should be effected. When I saw them reaching a decision I would get the right way up and quietly come down.

For a lot of children the best games are imaginary ones, by which everyday objects are transformed into the props of adventure. 'A Good Play' by Robert Louis Stevenson:

We built a ship upon the stairs
All made of the back-bedroom chairs,
And filled it full of sofa pillows
To go a-sailing on the billows.

We took a saw and several nails,
And water in the nursery pails;
And Tom said, 'Let us also take
An apple and a slice of cake;'
Which was enough for Tom and me
To go a-sailing on, till tea.

We sailed along for days and days,
And had the very best of plays;
But Tom fell out and hurt his knee,
So there was no one left but me.

One of the most popular forms of imaginary play is acting. But plays in single-sex schools always raise problems. A little poem by Mark Bevan – 'To a School Juliet':

Could I forget you in that other play,
     Then might your gentleness command belief
Nor present scenes be dulled by yesterday –
     With recollection muddied o'er. . .
                         In brief,
Sweet Capulet, I cannot overcome
The mem'ry of thee shoving in the scrum.

Sport has always been regarded as an essential part of education, building up the body with the mind, and certain sports have always carried social overtones. Here's a list of 'Courtly Exercises and Gentlemanlike Pastimes' recommended by Roger Ascham in the sixteenth century:

To ride comely: to run fair at tilt or ring: to play at all weapons: to shoot fair in bow, or surely in gun: to vault lustily: to run: to leap: to wrestle: to swim: to dance comely: to sing, and play instruments cunningly: to hawk: to hunt: to play tennis.

It's interesting that dancing was included in the list. Lord Chesterfield, writing to his son in 1745, also recommended it:

> My dear boy... Now that the Christmas breaking-up draws near, I have ordered Mr. Desnoyers to go to you, during that time, to teach you to dance. I desire you will particularly attend to the graceful motion of your arms; which, with the manner of putting on your hat, and giving your hand, is all that a gentleman need attend to. Dancing is in itself a very silly, trifling thing; but it is one of those established follies to which people of sense are sometimes obliged to conform; and they should be able to do it well. And, though I would not have you a dancer, yet, when you do dance, I would have you dance well, as I would have you do everything you do, well.

The pursuit of excellence is not the only argument in favour of sport in schools. Here is the view of Nigel Molesworth, the awful schoolboy created by Geoffrey Willans and Ronald Searle:

> Headmasters hav to hav some sort of excuse for games so that they can drive all boys and masters out into the foul and filthy air, while they stir the coals into a blaze and setle down with one of the gangster books they have confiskated.

Writers on the whole haven't been too keen on sport, and many remember that part of their schooldays with a shudder. John Betjeman recalls:

The dread of beatings! Dread of being late!
And, greatest dread of all, the dread of
games!

Another poet, W. B. Yeats:

I was useless at games. I cannot remember
that I ever kicked a goal or made a run.

The novelist, George Orwell, on football:

I loathed the game, and since I could see no
pleasure or usefulness in it, it was very
difficult for me to show courage at it. Football,
it seemed to me, is not really played for the

pleasure of kicking a ball about, but is a
species of fighting. The lovers of football are
large, boisterous, nobby boys who are good at
knocking down and trampling on slightly
smaller boys.

Cricket has its detractors too. It seems to offer no
middle course between the protracted tedium of a test
match and the squabbles of the family game. A little
poem by Hilaire Belloc, entitled 'The Game of Cricket':

I wish you'd speak to Mary, Nurse,
She's really getting worse and worse.
Just now when Tommy gave her out
She cried and then began to pout
And then she tried to take the ball
Although she cannot bowl at all.
And now she's standing on the pitch,
The miserable little Bitch!

All games are miserable when you don't know how to
play them or have no interest in them. In her book *My
Grandmothers and I*, Diana Holman-Hunt recalled her
introduction to tennis. As a child during the First
World War, she was invited to a tennis party by a Miss
Letty. Since she had no plimsolls, she was equipped
with a large pair of galoshes. But before they could
start playing, the court was marked out with pegs and
Diana was delegated to do the white lines:

I trudged round the lawn in my galoshes,

pushing the little white wheel. It was a
difficult task; there were so many pegs. I threw
my straw hat on the ground. I was sure Miss
Letty would be pleased with what I had done.

'Do come and see, it looks just like a Union
Jack!'

'Oh!' she cried, running towards me. 'What
have you done? There shouldn't be any
diagonal lines!'

Things don't get much better when they actually start
playing. A Major called Henry and his large daughter
Elsie arrive to make up the doubles match. They
prepare to play:

I stood still, holding my racquet before me. A
ball sailed over the net and landed in a cloud
of chalk. 'Line!' they cried, 'you must *run*!'

He biffed it again at Miss Letty; she
thrashed it back at Elsie, who tripped over a
peg and grazed her knee badly.

'Oh dear!' cried Miss Letty. 'That peg must
have been overlooked; I'm terribly sorry.'

She frowned. I wasn't sorry. It served Elsie
right.

Tennis parties don't happen so much nowadays, but
the institution of the children's party survives intact.
It remains the blessing of children and the bane of
parents. Here is a poem by Ogden Nash entitled
'Children's Party':

May I join you in the doghouse, Rover?
I wish to retire till the party's over.
Since three o'clock I've done my best
To entertain each tiny guest;
My conscience now I've left behind me,
And if they want me, let them find me.
I blew their bubbles, I sailed their boats,
I kept them from each other's throats.
I told them tales of magic lands,
I took them out to wash their hands.
I sorted their rubbers and tied their laces,
I wiped their noses and dried their faces.
Of similarity there's lots
'Twixt tiny tots and Hottentots.
I've earned repose to heal the ravages
Of these angelic-looking savages.
Oh, progeny playing by itself
Is a lonely fascinating elf,
But progeny in roistering batches
Would drive St. Francis from here to Natchez.
Shunned are the games a parent proposes;
They prefer to squirt each other with hoses.
Their playmates are their natural foemen
And they like to poke each other's abdomen.
Their joy needs another's woe to cushion it;
Say a puddle, and somebody littler to push in
    it.
They observe with glee the ballistic results
Of ice cream with spoons for catapults,

And inform the assembly with tears and
    glares
That everyone's presents are better than
    theirs.
Oh, little women and little men,
Someday I hope to love you again,
But not till after the party's over,
So give me the key to the doghouse, Rover.

I will close this chapter on play with a warning to all children – be careful what you play with. To reinforce the message here is an anonymous cautionary verse, 'Willie's Epitaph':

Little Willie from his mirror
   Licked the mercury right off,
Thinking, in his childish error,
   It would cure the whooping cough.
At the funeral his mother
   Smartly said to Mrs. Brown:
"Twas a chilly day for Willie
   When the mercury went down.'

5

work

The trouble with work is that it does go on rather. In the words of C. S. Lewis:

> Term, holidays, term, holidays, till we leave school, and then work, work, work till we die.

Slightly depressing. And of course it does rule out the possibility that you might actually enjoy doing it. Finley Peter Dunne:

> Work is work if you're paid to do it, and it's pleasure if you pay to be allowed to do it.

Jerome K. Jerome liked it:

> I like work; it fascinates me; I can sit and look at it for hours.

But what's difficult about work, whether for grown-

ups or children, is doing it at the right time. Robert Benchley:

> Anyone can do any amount of work provided it isn't the work he's supposed to be doing at that moment.

It's surprising how often work comes up in conversations with children. As you know, one of the commonest questions addressed to them is, What are you going to be when you grow up? In fact, it can be asked so often that it becomes positively boring. The answers to the question are more interesting, and they were the subject of some poems written by children and collected by Chris Searle. Here's one by Jackie Tolley:

> When I'm a man
>   I bet I can
> Climb a mountain and
>   Fly to Japan,

Ride every racing car,
 Ride into space
And finish my tea
Without jam on my face.

But you don't have to wait till you're in a job to start work. There always seems to be lots to do in every household, and children don't have to be very old before they get involved in it. Tidying up is usually the first work parents demand. Then come all those boring things like making beds and washing up, and from then on it doesn't really stop. In her book *My Grandmothers and I* Diana Holman-Hunt recalled one of them setting her to work:

> 'Now my dear, you can make yourself useful; there are many circulars, envelopes and paper bags ready on the Moorish throne.'
> 'Which do you need most, spills or lavatory paper?'
> 'Let me see – the latter I think, as none has been made for so long. Here is your knife. . . You will find the stiletto, the template and string in the Indian box over there.' She settled at the writing-table, and with a pin-like nib, scratched away at her letters.
> I ripped the blade through the stiff paper folded around the template. 'Some of these bags from Palmer's Stores are very thick and covered with writing.'
> 'Print is all right on one side you know. Try not to talk.'

When I had cut a hundred sheets, I pierced their corners and threaded them with a string; I tied this in a loop to hang on a nail by the 'Convenience'. I made a mental note of the softer pieces and put them together in the middle.

For many children work around the home is a way of augmenting their pocket money. In Hunter Davies's biography of the Beatles, John Lennon's aunt recalls the future pop star at the age of fourteen:

'I tried to teach him the value of money, but it never worked.'
To get any extra money, John had to work for it by helping in the garden.

'He always refused to, until he was really desperate. We'd hear the shed door being furiously opened, then he'd get the lawn-mower out and race across a few feet of lawn at about sixty miles an hour, then storm in for his money.'

The idea of children just working for pocket money is a fairly recent one. Until this century, a lot of very small children used to be sent out to do real work. Particularly in poor families, any contribution to their income was welcome. Children started work at a very early age. Here's Daniel Defoe's description of the cloth trade of Taunton in the 1720s:

One of the chief manufacturers of the town told us, that there was at that time so good a trade in the town, that they had then eleven hundred looms going . . .; and that which added to the thing very much, was, that not one of those looms wanted work. He farther added, that there was not a child in the town, or in the villages round it, of above five years old, but if it was not neglected by its parents, and untaught, could earn its own bread.

It's quite a thought, isn't it? – to have children self-supporting from the age of five. The work that they did varied enormously. In London a lot of children worked as street-traders. Henry Mayhew, in his huge social survey *London Labour and London Poor*, offered a reason why costermongers liked having boys to cry their wares:

Mostly the boy alone has to do this part of the work, the coster's voice being generally rough and hoarse, while the shrill sound of that of the boy re-echoes throughout the street along which they slowly move, and is far more likely to strike the ear, and, consequently to attract attention, than that of the man. This mode of 'practising the voice' is, however, perfectly ruinous to it, as in almost every case of this description we find the natural tone completely annihilated at a very early age, and a harsh, hoarse, guttural, disagreeable mode of speaking acquired.

Very few of these young street-traders would have had much education, but they would know enough to conduct their business. Mayhew interviewed an eight-year-old cress-seller on the subject:

I can't read or write, but I knows how many pennies goes to a shilling, why, twelve, of course, but I don't know how many ha'pence there is, though there's two to a penny. ... All my money I earns I puts in a club and draws it out for to buy clothes with. It's better than spending it on sweet-stuff, for them as has a living to earn. I ain't a child, and I shan't be a woman till I'm twenty, but I'm past eight, I am.

Children who had to go out to work so young must have had to grow up very fast and take on adult responsibilities very early. In Charles Dickens's *Bleak House* Mr Jarndyce and Esther Summerson meet three children in an attic. The eldest is a thirteen-year-old girl called Charley:

'And do you live alone here with these babies, Charley?' said my guardian.

'Yes, sir,' returned the child, looking up into his face with perfect confidence, 'since father died.'

'And how do you live, Charley? Oh! Charley,' said my guardian, turning his face away for a moment, 'how do you live?'

'Since father died, sir, I've gone out to work. I'm out washing to-day.'

'God help you, Charley!' said my guardian. 'You're not tall enough to reach the tub.'

'In pattens I am, sir,' she said quickly. 'I've got a high pair as belonged to mother.'

'And when did mother die? Poor mother!'

'Mother died, sir, just after Emma was born,' said the child, glancing at the face upon her bosom. 'Then father said I was to be as good a mother to her as I could. And so I tried. And so I worked at home, and did cleaning and nursing and washing, for a long time before I began to go out. And that's how I know how; don't you see sir?'

'And do you often go out?'

'As often as I can,' said Charley, opening her eyes, and smiling, 'because of earning sixpences and shillings!'

At least Charley – and indeed the street-traders – were working with a degree of freedom which children in factories didn't share. Here's an extract from John Aiken's *A Description of the Country from thirty to forty miles round Manchester*, published in 1795:

The invention and improvement of machines to shorten labour, has had surprising influence to extend our trade, and also to call in hands from all parts, especially children for the cotton mills. ... In these, children of very tender age are employed; many of them collected from the workhouses in London and Westminster, and transported in crowds, as apprentices to masters many hundreds of miles distant – where they serve, unknown, unprotected, and forgotten by those to whose care nature or the laws had consigned them.

Thomas Carlyle wrote:

All work, even cotton-spinning, is noble; work is alone noble.

But the way children were treated in the cotton mills was far from noble. So far as many of the mill-owners were concerned, they were just cheap labour. The American poet Don Marquis:

When a man tells you he got rich through hard work, ask him *whose?*

Because a lot of the factory-owners got rich by the hard work of their child workers, who couldn't complain very forcibly about the way they were treated. Exploitation of child labour went on for a very long time, even when there were laws to control it. Here's a reminiscence from Margaret Powell of working in a laundry early in this century:

When I got to be fifteen and was due for a
half a crown rise, I got the sack. They had no
need to pay you fifteen shillings a week. Girls
of fourteen could do what I was doing. So
that any excuse they found to get rid of you,
they did.

One of the best-known abuses of child labour in the
past was chimney-sweeping. In days before central
heating, every building was heated by open fires or
stoves, and, since there weren't any modern vacuum
pumps or even long collapsible brushes, the only way
to clean the chimneys was to send someone up there.
Since the chimneys were very narrow, that someone
had to be pretty small – in fact it had to be a child.
Many of the men who controlled these children were
very cruel and boys suffered terribly, working long
hours in appalling conditions.

The sweeps were very much part of the London scene. Here's the recollection of Charles Lamb, writing in 1823:

> When a child, what a mysterious pleasure it was to witness their operation! to see a chit no bigger than oneself enter, one knew not by what process, into what seemed the *Fauces Averni* (gates of hell) – to pursue him in imagination, as he went sounding on through so many dark stifling caverns, horrid shades! – to shudder with the idea that 'now, surely, he must be lost for ever'! – to revive at hearing his feeble shout of discovered daylight – and then (O fulness of delight) running out of doors, to come just in time to see the sable phenomenon emerge in safety, the brandished weapon of his art victorious like some flag waved over a conquered citadel! I seem to remember having been told, that a bad sweep was once left in a stack with his brush, to indicate which way the wind blew. It was an awful spectacle certainly . . .

Some children had a gentler introduction to the idea of work. Parents can certainly help young people to get used to the thought of it. Abraham Lincoln:

> My father taught me to work; he did not teach me to love it.

For many the first glimpse they get of work is a visit to their father's office or factory – which usually leads to a lot of bewildered wondering about what on earth he *does* there all day. John Betjeman used to be taken to look round his father's workshops:

> Bang through the packing room! Then up a
>   step:
> 'Be careful, Master John,' old William called.
> Over the silversmiths' uneven floor
> I thought myself a fast electric train,
> First stop the silver-plating shop (no time
> To watch the locksmiths' and engravers'
>   work):
> For there in silence Buckland used to drop
> Dull bits of metal into frothing tanks
> And bring them out all gold or silver bright –
> He'd turn a penny into half-a-crown.
> Though he but seldom spoke, yet he and I
> Worked there as one. He let me seem to
>   work.

But seeming to work is different from the tedium of real work. Some children have always found concentration difficult, and often they develop new ideas of their own as to how a job should be done. Here's an extract from Thomas Hardy's novel, *Jude the Obscure*. Young Jude is given the job of frightening birds off the farmer's crops:

The boy stood under the rick ... and every

92

few seconds used his clacker or rattle briskly.
At each clack the rooks left off pecking, and
rose and went away on their leisurely wings,
burnished like tassets of mail, afterwards
wheeling back and regarding him warily, and
descending to feed at a more respectful
distance.

He sounded the clacker till his arm ached,
and at length his heart grew sympathetic with
the birds' thwarted desires. They seemed, like
himself, to be living in a world which did not
want them. Why should he frighten them
away? They took upon them more and more
the aspect of gentle friends and pensioners –
the only friends he could claim as being the

93

least degree interested in him, for his aunt had often told him that she was not. He ceased his rattling, and they alighted anew.

'Poor little dears!' said Jude, aloud. 'You *shall* have some dinner – you shall. There is enough for us all. Farmer Troutham can afford to let you have some. Eat, then, my dear little birdies, and make a good meal!'

Starting work so young encouraged children to be independent and think for themselves. Here's a recollection from John Aubrey of the experimental philosopher, Robert Hooke:

When his father died, his Son Robert was but 13 yeares old, to whom he left one Hundred pounds, which was sent up to London with him, with an intention to have him bound Apprentice to Mr. Lilly the Paynter, with whom he was a little while upon tryall; who liked him very well, But Mr. Hooke quickly perceived what was to be donne, so, thought he, why cannot I doe this by my selfe and keepe my hundred pounds?

Exactly. There's a nice streak of independence in this reminiscence from William Cobbett, written in 1820. At the age of eleven he set off from Farnham to walk to Kew Gardens, where he hoped to get a job. He had thirteen half-pence in his pocket.

A long day (it was in June) brought me to Richmond in the afternoon. Twopennyworth of bread and cheese and a pennyworth of small beer which I had on the road, and one half-penny that I had lost somehow or other, left three pence in my pocket. With this for my whole fortune, I was trudging through Richmond in my blue smock-frock and my red garters tied under my knees, when, staring about me, my eye fell upon a little book in a bookseller's window, on the outside of which was written: 'TALE OF A TUB; Price 3d.' The title was so odd that my curiosity was excited. I had the 3d., but then I could have *no supper*. In I went and got the little book, which I was so impatient to read that I got over into a field, at the upper corner of Kew Gardens, where there stood a *hay-stack*.

. . . I read on till it was dark, without any thought of supper or bed. When I could see no longer I put my little book in my pocket, and tumbled down by the side of the stack, where I slept till the birds in Kew Gardens awakened me in the morning; when off I started to Kew, reading my little book. The singularity of my dress, the simplicity of my manner, my confident and lively air, and, doubtless, his own compassion besides, induced the gardener, who was a Scotsman, I remember, to give me victuals, find me lodging, and set me to work.

If you enjoy work it doesn't feel like work, but if you have to work on a day you had reckoned to be free it can seem very unjust. In Mark Twain's *Tom Sawyer*, Tom's aunt punishes him by making him paint her thirty-yard front fence. At first he is depressed by the prospect but then, when his friend Ben Rogers arrives, pretends he is enjoying it. Ben actually bribes Tom with an apple to let him have a go:

> Tom gave up the brush with reluctance in his face but alacrity in his heart. And while (Ben) worked and sweated in the sun, the retired artist sat on a barrel in the shade close by, dangled his legs, munched his apple, and planned the slaughter of more innocents. There was no lack of material; boys happened along every little while; they came to jeer, but remained to whitewash.
>
> By the time Ben was fagged out, Tom had traded the next chance to Billy Fisher for a kite, in good repair; and when *he* played out, Johnny Miller bought in for a dead rat and a string to swing it with; and so on, and so on, hour after hour. And when the middle of the afternoon came, from being a poor poverty-stricken boy in the morning, Tom was literally rolling in wealth. . . . He had had a nice, good idle time all the while – plenty of company – and the fence had three coats of whitewash on it! If he hadn't run out of whitewash, he would have bankrupted every boy in the village.

Tom said to himself that it was not such a hollow world, after all. He had discovered a great law of human action, without knowing it – namely, that in order to make a man or a boy covet a thing, it is only necessary to make the thing difficult to attain. If he had been a great and wise philosopher, like the writer of this book, he would have comprehended that Work consists of whatever a body is *obliged* to do, and that Play consists of whatever a body is not obliged to do.

Which sounds like a pretty good definition on which to end this chapter on work. Just one final thought from Don Herold:

Work is the greatest thing in the world, so we should always save some of it for tomorrow.

6

parents

The relationship between children and parents has always been a potentially stormy one. Here's Samuel Butler on the subject:

> Parents are the last people on earth who ought to have children.

Dorothy Parker:

> The best way to keep children home is to make the home atmosphere pleasant – and let the air out of the tires.

Oscar Wilde:

> Children begin by loving their parents. After a time they judge them. Rarely, if ever, do they forgive them.

John Wilmot, Earl of Rochester:

> Before I got married, I had six theories about
> bringing up children; now I have six children
> and no theories.

Very few parents and children get on well *all* the time.
It'd be pretty unnatural if they did. The most one can
hope is that parents and children should get on well
most of the time. They should, like trades unionists,
respect each other's differentials and work to negoti-
ate an acceptable settlement.

The basic principle that children should obey their
parents is a very old one, which recurs in most civiliza-
tions. Certainly it's recommended in the Bible:

> Honour thy father and mother: that thy days
> may be long upon the land which the Lord
> thy God giveth thee.

The religious message on the subject was sometimes pretty scary. Here's part of a sermon by John Wesley:

> Have you not been present when a father or mother has said, 'My child, do so or so'? The child, without any ceremony, answered peremptorily, 'I won't.' And the parent quietly passes it by, without any further notice. And does he or she not see, that, by this cruel indulgence, they are training up their child, by flat rebellion against their parents, to rebellion against God? Consequently they are training him up for the everlasting fire prepared for the devil and his angels! . . .
>
> This, therefore, I cannot but earnestly repeat – break their wills betimes; begin this great work before they can run alone, before they can speak plain, or perhaps speak at all. Whatever pains it cost, conquer their stubbornness; break the will, if you would not damn the child. I conjure you not to neglect, not to delay this! Therefore, (1) Let a child, from a year old, be taught to fear the rod and to cry softly. In order to this, (2) Let him have nothing he cried for; absolutely nothing, great or small; else you undo your own work. (3) At all events, from that age, make him do as he is bid, if you whip him ten times running to effect it. Let none persuade you it is cruelty to do this; it is cruelty not to do it. Break his will

now, and his soul will live, and he will probably bless you to all eternity.

Or alternatively he won't. One gets the feeling growing up can't have been much fun in those days. Writing a century earlier, in 1670, John Aubrey gave an equally dispiriting description of the relationship between children and parents:

> The gentry and citizens had little learning of any kind, and their way of breeding their children was suitable to the rest. They were as severe to their children as their schoolmasters; and their schoolmasters as masters of the house of correction. The child perfectly loathed the sight of his parents as the slave his torture.

Needless to say, that sort of upbringing didn't make children and parents very close. Another, rather sad, little snippet of Aubrey, writing about his adolescence:

> My father sent me into the country again: where I conversed with none but servants and rustics and soldiers quartered, to my great grief, for in those days fathers were not acquainted with their children. It was a most sad life to me, then in the prime of my youth, not to have the benefit of an ingenious Conversation and scarcely any good books.

So obedience and respect were the rule; disobedience and disrespect were punished severely. The punishments often took very practical form. This is what Charles Seymour, the sixth Duke of Somerset, did in about 1700:

> 'The Proud Duke' (as he was known) made his two daughters stand guard over him while he took his afternoon nap and, on waking to find one of them sitting down, docked £20,000 from her inheritance.

And in those days £20,000 really was £20,000. Yes, wherever you turned, the message was loud and clear – obey your parents – or else. In 1715, Isaac Watts brought out his *Divine and Moral Songs for Children*. Here's the one on 'Obedience to Parents':

Let Children that would fear the Lord
  Hear what their teachers say
With rev'rence meet their parents' word
  And with delight obey.

Have we not heard what dreadful plagues
  Are threatened by the Lord
To him that breaks his father's law
  Or mocks his mother's word?

What heavy guilt upon him lies!
  How cursed is his name!
The ravens shall pick out his eyes
  And eagles eat the same.

But those that worship God, and give
  Their parents honour due
Here on this Earth they long shall live
  And live hereafter too.

The children who didn't rebel against all this heavy moral propaganda must have been, by our standards, joyless little goody-goodies. Here's an extract from John Ruskin's *Praeterita*, in which he describes his upbringing in the early nineteenth century:

We seldom had company, even on weekdays; and I was never allowed to come down to dessert, until much later in life – when I was able to crack nuts neatly. I was then permitted

to come down to crack other people's nuts for them – (I hope they liked the ministration) – but never to have any myself; nor anything else of dainty kind, either then or at other times. Once at Hunter Street, I recollect my mother giving me three raisins, in the forenoon, out of the store cupboard; and I remember perfectly the first time I tasted custard ... My father was dining in the front room, and did not finish his custard; and my mother brought me the bottom of it into the back room.

Ruskin was not really writing with disapproval of such an upbringing, but he could not help observing the effect that sort of awestruck respect for parents had:

I had nothing to love ... My parents were –
in a sort – visible powers of nature to me, no
more loved than the sun and moon: only I
should have been annoyed and puzzled if
either of them had gone out.

The danger of parents setting themselves up on such
pedestals is that, for the child, there must inevitably
come a terrible moment of disillusionment. This has
rarely been better described than by Edmund Gosse in
his memoir of his own grim childhood, *Father and Son*:

> I confused him in some sense with God; at all
> events I believed that my father knew
> everything and saw everything. One morning
> in my sixth year, my mother and I were alone
> in the morning room, when my father came in
> and announced some fact to us. I was
> standing on the rug, gazing at him, and when

he made this statement, I remember turning quickly, in embarrassment, and looking into the fire. The shock to me was as that of a thunderbolt, for what my father had said *was not true*. Here was the appalling discovery, never suspected before, that my father was not as God, and did not know everything.

All children start by thinking that their parents know everything, but sensible parents let them down gently into the realization we're all just fallible human beings. Only foolish parents will go on trying to convince their children they know everything, and only very foolish parents will punish their children for not believing them.

Mind you, every parent has to come to terms with some sort of punishment. I'm afraid the child hasn't yet been born who's good all the time (and that's just as well, because I don't think he or she would be very nice to know). But attitudes to punishment vary. Bishop Fulton J. Sheen:

Every child should have an occasional pat on the back, as long as it is applied low enough and hard enough.

Most systems of upbringing which completely eliminate punishment run into trouble. There's one described in *Mother's Helper*, a recent book by Maureen Freely. Laura, the helper of the title, joins a family run by the very modern mother, Kay Pyle:

106

On three or four occasions, when the children had fights and refused to resolve them as their mother suggested, Kay took one of them upstairs with her for a good think.

When Laura actually finds where the children go to do their thinking it's rather a shock. She goes upstairs to find four-year-old Nathaniel, who is having a good think:

The Thinking Room was a closet. It was the only room in the house without an intercom. It had been fitted out with blankets and furry cushions and, although there was no lock on the door (only some grooves for a padlock), it was difficult to open and close . . . She fumbled for the light switch and when she found it, no light went on. Looking up, she saw that the bulb, if there ever had been one, had been removed from the socket. Nathaniel whimpered and buried his face in the cushions.

It sounds just like a modern variation on the old punishment of locking a child up in a cupboard or room. Just as the young Jane Eyre, in Charlotte Brontë's book, was locked up for her sins in the red room:

'Besides,' said Miss Abbott, 'God will punish her. He might strike her dead in the midst of her tantrums, and then where would she go?

Come, Bessie, we will leave her: I wouldn't
have her heart for anything. Say your prayers,
Miss Eyre, when you are by yourself; for if
you don't repent, something bad might be
permitted to come down the chimney and
fetch you away.'

   They went, shutting the door, and locking it
behind them.

There's still something very chilling about that. But
some of the old parental threats have lost a bit of force
in modern times. A thought from Sam Levenson:

Remember when your mother used to say, 'Go to your room –'? This was a terrible penalty. Now when a mother says the same thing, a kid goes to his room. There he's got an air-conditioner, a TV set, an intercom, a short-wave radio – he's better off than he was in the first place.

Mind you, it's what used to happen to children before they got sent to their rooms which was awful. Let's now have a piece about a really awful Victorian father, Mr Theobald Pontifex. He was created by Samuel Butler in *The Way of All Flesh* and I'm afraid there were real parents like him. The narrator of the book is spending Sunday with the Pontifex family:

> In the course of the evening (the children) came into the drawing-room, and, as an especial treat, were to sing some of their hymns to me, instead of saying them, so that I might hear how nicely they sang. Ernest was to choose the first hymn, and he chose one about some people who were to come to the sunset tree. I am no botanist, and do not know what kind of tree a sunset tree is, but the words began, 'Come, come, come; come to the sunset tree for the day is past and gone.' The tune was rather pretty and had taken Ernest's fancy, for he was unusually fond of music and had a sweet little child's voice which he liked using.

109

He was, however, very late in being able to sound a hard 'c' or 'k', and, instead of saying 'Come,' he said 'Tum, tum, tum.'

'Ernest,' said Theobald, from the arm-chair in front of the fire, where he was sitting with his hands folded before him, 'don't you think it would be very nice if you were to say "come" like other people, instead of "tum"?'

'I do say tum,' replied Ernest, meaning that he said 'come'.

Theobald was always in a bad temper on Sunday evening. Whether it is that they are as much bored with the day as their neighbours, or whether they are tired, or whatever the cause may be, clergymen are seldom at their best on Sunday evening; I had already seen signs that evening that my host was cross, and was a little nervous at hearing Ernest say so promptly 'I do say tum', when his papa had said he did not say it as he should.

Theobald noticed the fact that he was being contradicted in a moment. He got up from his arm-chair and went to the piano.

'No, Ernest, you don't,' he said, 'you say nothing of the kind, you say "tum", not "come". Now say "come" after me, as I do.'

'Tum,' said Ernest at once. 'Is that better?' I have no doubt he thought it was, but it was not.

'Now, Ernest, you are not taking pains: you are not trying as you ought to do. It is high time you learned to say "come", why, Joey can say "come", can't you, Joey?'

'Yeth, I can,' replied Joey, and he said something which was not far off 'come'.

'There, Ernest, do you hear that? There's no difficulty about it, nor shadow of difficulty. Now, take your own time, think about it, and say "come" after me.'

The boy remained silent for a few seconds and then said 'tum' again.

I laughed, but Theobald turned to me impatiently and said, 'Please do not laugh, Overton; it will make the boy think it does not matter, and it matters a great deal;' then

turning to Ernest, he said, 'Now, Ernest, I will give you one more chance, and if you don't say "come", I shall know that you are self-willed and naughty.'

He looked very angry, and a shade came over Ernest's face, like that which comes upon the face of a puppy when it is being scolded without understanding why. The child saw well what was coming now, was frightened, and, of course, said 'tum' once more.

'Very well, Ernest,' said his father, catching him angrily by the shoulder, 'I have done my best to save you, but if you will have it so, you will,' and he lugged the little wretch, crying by anticipation, out of the room. A few minutes more and we could hear screams coming from the dining-room, across the hall which separated the drawing-room from the dining-room, and knew that poor Ernest was being beaten.

'I have sent him to bed,' said Theobald, as he returned to the drawing-room, 'and now, Christina, I think we will have the servants in to prayers,' and he rang the bell for them, red-handed as he was.

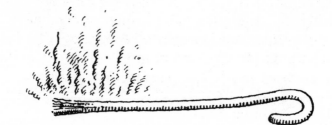

When you hear something like that, you feel that some people just aren't qualified to be parents. George Bernard Shaw agreed:

> Parentage is a very important profession; but no test of fitness for it is ever imposed in the interest of children.

So far in this chapter, actually, there hasn't been much 'in the interest of children'. It's mostly been about the obedience which parents have demanded of their offspring. But what one has to remember is that children are not naturally obedient or respectful. Here's a memory of King George II:

> One night while the Queen was ill, as he was sitting in his nightgown and nightcap in a great chair, with his legs upon a stool, and nobody in the room with him but the Princess Emily, who lay upon a couch, and Lord Hervey, who sat by the fire, he talked . . . of his own courage in the storm and his illness, till the Princess Emily, as Lord Hervey thought, fell fast asleep. . . . The King, turning towards Princess Emily, and seeing her eyes shut, cried: 'Poor good child! her duty, affection, and attendance on her mother have quite exhausted her spirits.' And soon after he went into the Queen's room.
>   As soon as his back was turned, Princess Emily started up, and said: 'Is he gone? Jesus! How tiresome he is!'

Some children not only show disrespect for their parents, they also boss them about. A remark by the late Duke of Windsor:

> The thing that impresses me most about America is the way parents obey their children.

And one from Oscar Wilde:

> Fathers should be neither seen nor heard; that is the only proper basis for family life.

Unfair to parents. Let's have a little comfort from Gwen Raverat:

> You may take it from me, that however hard you try – or don't try; whatever you do – or don't do; for better, for worse; for richer, for poorer; every way and every day:
> THE PARENT IS ALWAYS WRONG.
> So it is no good bothering about it. When the little pests grow up they will certainly tell you exactly what you did wrong in their case. But never mind; they will be just as wrong themselves in their turn.

The relationship between parent and child starts with birth. Some parents reckon the earliest years are the easiest, before the child can answer back. Certainly there's something nice about babies. Robert Southey:

114

A house is never perfectly furnished for
enjoyment unless there is a child in it rising
three years old, and a kitten rising three
weeks.

But babies bring their problems for parents. Leo J.
Burke:

People who say they sleep like a baby usually
don't have one.

And as children get older, they can still be rather a
hindrance to their parents, particularly when there's
work to be done. Thomas Hood set out the problem
very well in his 'Parental Ode to My Son, Aged 3 Years
and 5 Months':

Thou happy, happy elf!
(But stop – first let me kiss away that tear) –
Thou tiny image of myself!
(My love, he's poking peas into his ear!)
Thou merry, laughing sprite!
With spirits feather-light,
Untouch'd by sorrow, and unsoiled by sin –
(Good heavens! the child is swallowing a pin!)

Thou little tricksy Puck!
With antic toys so funnily bestuck,
Light as the singing bird that wings the air –
(The door! the door! he'll tumble down the
    stair!)
Thou darling of thy sire!
(Why, Jane, he'll set his pinafore a-fire!)
Thou imp of mirth and joy!
In Love's dear chain so strong and bright a
    link,
Thou idol of thy parents – (Drat the boy!
There goes my ink!)

Thou cherub – but of earth –
Fit playfellow for Fays, by moonlight pale,
In harmless sport and mirth,
(That dog will bite him if he pulls his tail!)
Thou human humming-bee, extracting
    honey
From ev'ry blossom in the world that blows,
Singing in Youth's Elysium ever sunny,
(Another tumble! – that's his precious nose!)

Thy father's pride and hope!
(He'll break the mirror with that
      skipping-rope!)
With pure heart newly stamped from Nature's
      mint –
(Where *did* he learn that squint?)
   Thou young domestic dove!
(He'll have that jug off, with another shove!)
   Dear nursling of the hymeneal nest!
   (Are those torn clothes his best?)
   Little epitome of man!
(He'll climb upon the table, that's his plan!)
Touch'd with the beauteous tints of dawning
      life –
   (He's got a knife!)

   Thou enviable being!
No storms, no clouds, in thy blue sky
      foreseeing,
   Play on, play on,
   My elfin John!
Toss the light ball – bestride the stick –
(I knew so many cakes would make him sick!)
With fancies, bouyant as the thistle-down,
Prompting the face grotesque, and antic brisk,
   With many a lamb-like frisk,
(He's got the scissors, snipping at your gown!)

   Thou pretty opening rose!
(Go to your mother, child, and wipe your
      nose!)

Balmy and breathing music like the South,
(He really brings my heart into my mouth!)
Fresh as the morn, and brilliant as its star –
(I wish that window had an iron bar!)
Bold as the hawk, yet gentle as the dove –
    (I'll tell you what, my love,
I cannot write, unless he's sent above!)

Mothers are traditionally supposed to have more patience with small children than fathers. I'm not sure that they actually do; I think it's just a role that's forced on them. But a lot of mothers do get gooey over babies. Dr Johnson didn't approve of this. A recollection by John Timbs:

> As Dr. Johnson was riding in a carriage through London on a rainy day, he overtook a poor woman carrying a baby, without any protection from the weather. Making the driver stop the coach, he invited the poor woman to get in with her child, which she did. After she had seated herself, the Doctor said to her:- 'My good woman, I think it most likely that the motion of the coach will wake your child in a little while, and I wish you to understand that if you talk any baby-talk to it, you will have to get out of the coach.' As the Doctor had anticipated, the child soon awoke, and the forgetful mother exclaimed to it:- 'Oh! the little dear, is he going to open his *eyesy-pysy*?' 'Stop the coach, driver!' shouted

Johnson; and the woman had to get out, and finish her journey on foot.

You can't expect outsiders to have the same appreciation of children as parents do. Mothers, in particular. Mothers do all kinds of things for their children, even write poems for them. Here's one written by Mary Barber in the early eighteenth century. It's called 'Written for my Son, and Spoken by Him at His First Putting on Breeches':

What is it our mammas bewitches,
To plague us little boys with breeches?
To tyrant Custom we must yield
Whilst vanquished Reason flies the field.
Our legs must suffer by ligation,
To keep the blood from circulation;

119

And then our feet, though young and tender,
We to the shoemaker surrender;
Who often makes our shoes so strait
Our growing feet they cramp and fret;
Whilst, with contrivance most profound,
Across our insteps we are bound;
Which is the cause, I make no doubt,
Why thousands suffer in the gout.
Our wiser ancestors wore brogues,
Before the surgeons bribed these rogues,
With narrow toes, and heels like pegs,
To help to make us break our legs.
Then, ere we know to use our fists,
Our mothers closely bind our wrists;
And never think our clothes are neat,
Till they're so tight we cannot eat.
And, to increase our other pains,
The hat-band helps to cramp our brains.
The cravat finishes the work,
Like bowstring sent from the Grand Turk.

Thus dress, that should prolong our date,
Is made to hasten on our fate.

You see, children have always been complaining
about the hoops their parents make them jump
through. But very few parents can help being ambitious for their children – though they may be wiser not
to. Here's a poem written in the eleventh century by
Su Tung-P'o. It was translated from the Chinese by
Arthur Waley and is called 'On the Birth of His Son':

Families, when a child is born
Want it to be intelligent.
I, through intelligence,
Having wrecked my whole life,
Only hope the baby will prove
Ignorant and stupid.
Then he will crown a tranquil life
By becoming a Cabinet Minister.

And that's about it for parents. I'll close with an even older thought. This one comes from about 150 B.C. and is quoted by Diogenes Laertius:

When asked why he did not become a father, Thales answered: 'Because I am fond of children.'

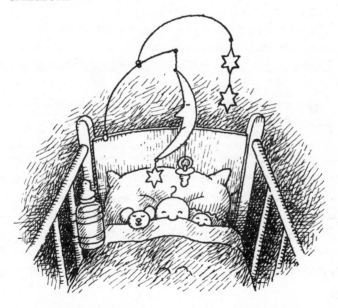

acknowledgements

Permission from authors and publishers to quote from the following works is gratefully acknowledged: 'Sonny Boy' by P. G. Wodehouse from *Eggs, Beans and Crumpets* (Herbert Jenkins); *The Diaries of Evelyn Waugh* (Weidenfeld and Nicolson); 'Quiet Fun' by Harry Graham from *Most Ruthless Rhymes for Heartless Homes*; 'Don't Cry Darling, It's Blood All Right' from *Family Reunion* and 'Children's Party' by Ogden Nash (J. M. Dent & Sons Ltd), reproduced by permission of the Estate of Ogden Nash, *Verses from 1929 On* by Ogden Nash Copyright 1934, 1935 by the Curtis Publishing Company, 'Don't Cry Darling, It's Blood All Right' first appeared in the *Saturday Evening Post*, 1934 and 'Children's Party' first appeared in the *Saturday Evening Post*, 1935, by permission of Little, Brown and Company; 'The Godfather and His Godchild' by James Thurber, © *Vintage Thurber Volume II* Copyright 1963 Hamish Hamilton; Copr. © 1950 James Thurber. Copr. © 1978 Helen W. Thurber and Rosemary Thurber Sauers. From *Further Fables for Our Time*, published by Simon & Schuster; *How to be Topp* by Geoffrey Willans and Ronald Searle (Max Parrish); 'Charles Augustus Fortescue' from *Cautionary Tales* by Hilaire Belloc (Duckworth & Co. Ltd); 'The Hell at Pooh Corner' from *Golfing For Cats* by Alan Coren (Robson Books); 'The Love That Purifies' by P. G. Wodehouse from *Very Good, Jeeves*; 'Theobald James' and 'Now We Are Sick' by J. B. Morton from *Beachcomber – the Works of J. B. Morton* (Frederick Muller); *Cider With Rosie* by Laurie Lee (Hogarth Press); *Bunter Does His Best* by Frank Richards (Cassell); *Akenfield* by Ronald Blythe (Penguin); *My Early Life* by W. S. Churchill, reproduced by permission of the Hamlyn Publishing Group Ltd; *And Now All This* by W. C. Sellar and R. J. Yeatman (Methuen); 'The Game of Cricket' by Hilaire Belloc from *Selected Letters of Hilaire Belloc*, reprinted by permission of A. D. Peters & Co. Ltd; *My Grandmothers and I* by Diana Holman Hunt (Hamish Hamilton); *Lessons in the Varsity of Life* by Lord Baden Powell, reproduced by permission of the Hamlyn Publishing Group Ltd; *Autobiography of Bertrand Russell* (Allen & Unwin); 'To a School Juliet' by Mark Bevan, reproduced by permission of Punch; *Essays: Such, Such Were the Joys* by George Orwell, reproduced by permission of Mrs Sonia Brownell Orwell and Martin Secker & Warburg; Poem by Jackie Tolley from *Stepney Words* (Vol. II) (Reality Press); 'Summoned by Bells' by John Betjeman (John Murray); *Below Stairs* by Margaret Powell (Peter Davies); *The Beatles* by Hunter Davies (Heinemann); *Mother's Helper* by Maureen Freely (Jonathan Cape); Excerpted from the book *Mother's Helper* by Maureen Freely. Copyright © 1979 by Maureen Freely. Reprinted by permission of Delacorte Press/Seymour Lawrence. *Period Piece – A Cambridge Childhood* by Gwen Raverat, reprinted by permission of Faber and Faber; 'On the Birth of His Son' by Su Tung P'o translated by Arthur Waley from *170 Chinese Poems* (Constable).